Praise for *Daughters of Harriet*

"*Daughters of Harriet* is both praise song and eulogy, as Cynthia Parker-Ohene explores the continuum of Black women's survival. Although her regional touchstones might briefly locate readers in place, she collapses time to show how past horrors still live in the present, how 'savageBlackgrrrls [may] buckle' no matter where they are in history. In these poems, Parker-Ohene paints these fraught narratives with imagery as fragrant and delicious as 'sweet peas butter beans the sachets of lavender roses,' creating a striking juxtaposition that will keep readers returning to this debut collection."

—*Chet'la Sebree,* author of *Field Study* and *Mistress*

"Parker-Ohene writes me into a past as rich and immersive as Octavia Butler's writings of the future—a past when I taste, smell, and feel underfoot the labor to live. Harriet Tubman makes the bone of this book. She is the embodiment of ancestry, the 'trace and aura in the head of my head.' Blackness is not hidden in this book but celebrated—'Forgotten Negroes: Hospital for the Negro Insane' announces Blackness by listing the contents of a suitcase: 'negro baby shoes, negro starter gun, 2 negro letters to kin in West Virginia.' Parker-Ohene provokes me to ask: what do I carry when my Black body is endangered? This poet gives me a historical guide to follow on my way through, if not my way out of, others' designs."

—*CM Burroughs,* author of *Master Suffering* and *The Vital System*

"Cynthia Parker-Ohene's 'mad song' is sung from one place that touches everywhere. The 'Black clarities' that build the song occur not purely as a sonic happening, but as a private world of being, a moment to swoon and sashay amongst the pines. *Daughters of Harriet* is an anatemporal cistern for pleasure, irreverence, and memory that invites the reader to enter into the wild lineage of those who walked on water, whose crossing meant a rupture in language. Ohene speaks from that rupture with righteous derision and humor, though the speaking is more akin to an incantation that reanimates those Black stories lost in the slip of time."

—*Taylor Johnson,* author of *Inheritance*

Daughters

– of –

Harriet

The Mountain West Poetry Series
Stephanie G'Schwind, Donald Revell, Kazim Ali,
Dan Beachy-Quick & Camille T. Dungy
series editors

CYNTHIA PARKER-OHENE

Daughters

– of –

Harriet

poems

The Center for Literary Publishing
Colorado State University

For information about permission to reproduce
selections from this book, write to
Permissions
The Center for Literary Publishing
9105 Campus Delivery
Colorado State University
Fort Collins, Colorado 80523-9105.

Printed in the United States of America.

Credits: "Portrait of Harriet Tubman," page 2, by Benjamin F. Powelson, 1868 (Library of Congress).
The title "Then I Will Speak on the Ashes," page 8, is borrowed from Sojourner Truth's *Narrative of
Sojourner Truth: Book of Life,* 1875. The title "act so there is no use in a centre," page 39, is borrowed
from Gertrude Stein's *Tender Buttons,* 1914. "Photograph of Harriet Tubman," page 67,
photographer unknown, 1911 (Library of Congress).

Library of Congress Cataloging-in-Publication Data

Names: Parker-Ohene, Cynthia, author.
Title: Daughters of Harriet : poems / Cynthia Parker-Ohene.
Other titles: Mountain west poetry series.
Description: Fort Collins : The Center for Literary Publishing, [2022] |
Series: The Mountain west poetry series
Identifiers: LCCN 2021050292 (print) | LCCN 2021050293 (ebook) | ISBN
9781885635815 (paperback) | ISBN 9781885635822 (ebook)
Subjects: LCSH: African American women--Poetry. | African
Americans--Poetry. | LCGFT: Poetry.
Classification: LCC PS3616.A7528 D38 2022 (print) | LCC PS3616.A7528
(ebook) | DDC 811/.6--dc23
LC record available at https://lccn.loc.gov/2021050292
LC ebook record available at https://lccn.loc.gov/2021050293

The paper used in this book meets the minimum requirements of
the American National Standard for Information Sciences-Permanence of Paper
for Printed Library Materials, ANSI Z39.48-1984.

Publication of this book was made possible by a grant from
the National Endowment for the Arts.

ART WORKS.

National
Endowment
for the Arts
arts.gov

For my great-grandmother Lucinda Curry,
my grandmother Mary Curry Kelley,
and especially my mother, Dorothy Beatrice Kelley (Parker),
my daughter, Briana Ohene, and my grandson, Bear

Contents

If you are silent about your pain, they'll kill you and say you enjoyed it.
— Zora Neale Hurston, *Their Eyes Were Watching God*

Daughters

– of –

Harriet

forced beds

corner a dysmembered self

    odd nails clamps juju dreams

        insurrection swoons a coy note

                the mad song   interrupts

Grrrl Black in Kilmarnock

My grandmother sets the table for our morning meal with squash blossoms, smudges of butter, fried porgies and corn, and a tumbler of iced tea. My grandmother drops vine-wrought lavender into the tumbler and there is a faint smell of maple wafting through the screen. I quickly wash up in the enamel basin.

She weaponizes silence so we quickly chant the prayers we have been taught since we began to walk. I mention something about bless the food we are about to eat, and I forget the rest. She looks at me with the evil eye and I close my eyes in deference to Jesus.

Monocacy River and my grandfather the fisherman who owns the land that they toil comes in from his dawn's work with a satchel of porgies, oyster trout and is preparing to leave to search for blue crabs. I follow him into his day waiting to swing from his thick arms and I holler with joy. My grandfather says that I can toss the food scraps into the trough where I am filled with glee at the tussling of hogs for the large bits of mixed leftovers. I am visiting from New York City and mesmerized by the old pickup. I sit in the bed of the truck and wave furiously to our kith who are ginning their wares for market.

My grandmother bought me a bow and arrow that keeps me deliriously happy. My mother admonishes her for buying such a dangerous boy toy. I have a good aim. She's afraid that I will kill myself or put out an eye.

Kilmarnock is my mother's home. My father is from the landside of percolation ponds near the South Carolina border and my mother says that it is too south even though she is from Virginia. My father and I exchange a wicked glance and my mother sucks her teeth.

Summers in the South are where Black children domiciled in the large cities that our parents went to during the Great Migration. Its farmlands are Black spaces for us to be free from the surveillance of Black lives.

We make pails of ice cream and play red light green light well into the dark. At home we run home at dusk right before the streetlights come on. I look for fireflies for my mason jar and croon at the marquee effect of their shine. I feel safe on the farm unaware that we are neither accepted nor welcomed here.

We are shielded from the history of our plight and we swing out from makeshift swings of old tires chasing chicks and roosters. I am allowed to touch what I see. I play the untuned piano in the parlor and yodel my favorite songs. I can still see them in the large white house on a creek filled with crabs and fish in the house where my mother was delivered by the midwife, her auntie Teal my grandmother's older sister. I am the last one.

Prevalence of Ritual

after a painting by Romare Bearden

these women
these salteaters
purl untucked sheets leftover from baptism
reset a paraffin lamp recessed in lichen
a perched daguerreotype atop
a scarred chifforobe
clutches an unknown grrrl standing beside
trumpeter swans
the inscription reads lucinda 1879 kilmarnock
its wings appear to cloak her hairline forming a muted halo
but it's only the birthing caul
she came seeing an already
the camera angles her brand
she's wearing a loose burnoose shawl
from potato sacks
crushed glass beneath her left foot
shines nacre from her shore
borrowed from turtle island
on the back of the frameless capture
a scrawl "somma dem bones is mine"

Daughters of Harriet

her memory of running
through sweet birch
and sinewy montane soils
sound to sea

the madding sway
obscures degradations of menstrual
moons   the otoliths of suffering
in its clitoral moments pulse

marcelled garnets beneath the razor of home and
unhomed recalled its whiteness of heat blears
sundered women beneath the coals of slaves
the odd nails of hate lie within the politics of God

the swift rub of soured nettles
African marigolds in conjure bags
the talc of skippers and the salt of brown rivers
of balm   a sash across the quivering sheath

she believes in the benevolence of terrible things
her body's serfdom   bitten mirages   the collateral of skin that
shellacs the wretched earth in Black clarities
and the memory of running beginning again and again

Then I Will Speak on the Ashes

This is a story about borders and migrations When the rains fall in the sea organs blacken reservoirs of drinking water we sort and dry the rows of derelict greens cracked fauna now cisterns on the margins of wooden houses its lines of vulnerability transform into arks as the weather turns on us The grounds absorb the trauma of drooping foliage Impotent gris-gris no longer potion or whirs into the waste of human industry Our food is the bloodied livestock its spoils leave hunger in the zephyr We try to replace what we lost among the rows of derelict limbs uniformed membranes the cauterized eye of the storm unseeding grains the white resin of starvation the flutter tonguing from the dry folds of their undersides The last sweet remembrances of dates and cassava No daily bread solely the chewed meat of skeletal petals its ligatures of hunger white as asp in the faun The slithering tongues color the scab what prophecy Amistad is a revelation snuffed I hear these tabernacles can't blood a she song Bring flight will sea? more scab than skin spears I want it Black Crime it here in this crystal jar Liberation I have always been here my overgotten The lived that relive cannot she freedoms jungled confessions a coating of damaged pedaling away to the volatile sublight she a constellation of widowed cities Yet she barren a disappearing lake Darkness ways be light   she-reflections   she skiffs the lip of damaged estuaries in red seas of reduction Shock in the layers of ruboff Memories confess snubbed essences of wrong loves Found in barbs of flowers a fen through the mesh of midcollapse There she be a woman with hair of thatched palms buoyant in a working wagon with a bottleneck of blue fibers an upstream porch nested with water ghosts in pitched tents she carried lints of corpses from tubs of riverrain on her skin she is a gutterwoman these voices spit knuckled only by a colored woman's reminiscents that spawned her Black nerves

Erasures of History

A hewer of wood separates a guild of disordered potions

Below a drawer of water sifts drowned carcasses of placenta reds

Each forms a mettled ghee

Under her bed she places forsythias of spilled mares

Olden pictures without frames

A sieve of shifting circumstances rests on a table of mirrors

Dysmembering forced migrations

My Mother the Lunch Lady

Each day at 8 a.m., my mother the lunch lady works the assembly line of newly made meals each a stamp of mass, scratched from the unlimited land of heather and sunflower risings.

She reaches home at 3, after a day of patriarchy whose offspring depend on her, to be coddled, each her presumed favorite. A maid at school. Her face erased from her colored, marked body—universally misseen, misnamed.

After school, I watch her, in her bedroom, removing her school clothes, collecting her uniforms for the wash. Her handkerchief shaped like a doily on her uniform's lapel, with the name Dot inside. I don't know her as this woman, a Blackwoman whose birth is tied up in her labor. She labors for the small coins, to use her Blackbody as surrogate for elevated white women, who

insist she nourish what their whiteness has wrought. Manage their childish fears, miss anne said, be hattie, be the wind, be mammy for 8 hours while they are in preparation for future domination. They have the power my mother could not imagine. At home Dot is taking what is not really quiet time, but in the slimmest of single moments, within the enclosing generational chasm of servitude and place, in these moments she belongs to no one.

She says it is her nerves; she needs ("unrespected" moments) to fight for her life in a life, where she is owned by the state, her husband, her daughters, the church, the community, who say that she is the very nice lady with a smile who exists to serve lunch at this unintegrated school. The lunch lady with cancer, cancer that silenced, sank her until she retreated with her voice. The labor, the Blackfemalebody she couldn't corral, but succumbed, when home meant gone.

potters' field

in the throat of crownsville, maryland
beneath the filament of pine and tobacco
reedy blue asters outline the old prison cottage
for colored women
            held in parch and punishment

                    forensics is memory

a sash of light from the monocacy river   arcs BELOVED   while maddish seasons
dismember her station hulled beneath the muck   turned livid   on the edges of things
like vindictive weeds or nervous trees   a caste even unto death
            as though bone may copulate with bone

The History of Gynecology

The enslavers cage the Black grrrls first
They lop off the braiding and fingernails, which they
place in a clamped gunnysack with oddments:
nettings, peeled eyes, negro repellant, disintegrated limbs,
and assorted mason jars teeming with enslaved menstrual blood,

and scraped labia wounds for surveillance, dr. sims
slashes the whistling gorges in the experiments he loved, the way
a hottentot scorches in a frankincense of fistulas draping the
operating table Only savageBlackgrrrls possess a hottentot
These savageBlackgrrrls buckle under the tup of
dismemberment

an unbraiding of the feminine, the braiding dr sims thought baroque, an
aboriginal juju The elongated tufts from the Blacksavagegrrrls' pre-owned
hottentot, now, fur pelts dressed the shoulders of his waltzing wife on alpine
nights, while Blackgrrrls these savageBlackgrrrls, Lucy, Anarcha, and Betsey—
who possessed a mauled and ethereal hottentot—prepared

mistress's hibiscus tea and teacakes However, mistress sims wanted
something more She inquired about these savageBlackgrrrls' hottentots,
about the incense of the hottentot She wanted to rub it across her vagina to
entice and woman, mistress sims craved the smell of the hottentot

An African primrose the Blacksavagegrrrls possessed, such Blacksavagegrrrls, Lucy,
17, Anarcha, and Betsey, both 18, did not avow pain, because they lived through
the fear of an ensnared fetal skull gashed in the birth canal, along with insertions of
tinned speculums If savageBlackgrrrls felt the terrorism of

bloodletting, it was not known to them The surgical apartheid covens
continued to peel back each bark of Black skin, an antebellum monogram
whittled into a napalm whorl Their imperialized hottentots on oppression tables
as a storehouse of balm for white women among lacy sawn and portland stone
This, under the cedar cladding, on the landside of percolation ponds, canted
bays, crossing coves and arched lunettes held by doric piers with the burnt smell
of hottentot and yaa

weather report

boots mean mud from the kilmarnock shore buckeyed oyster trout and salty blue crabs
carried in under uncle william's red slicker from his fishing boat appear on steamy plates
of colored-made food in a 1921 white stucco house with 3 missing steps and a parked
horse-drawn carriage driven illegally by the colored owner in a colored enclave near
lancaster county virginia the land they lived on thought to be barren by previous owners
was deeded to william kelley but moisture from his bark appeared several grandchildren
beyond the white stucco with 3 missing steps sits under a drapery of willow wisps and
pink cottonwoods follow a pollen path of papillon beadings scattered petals and yucca
casts sometimes sun wife of moon spreads fodder to feed for 9 fortnights at a time.
its dawn and dewy earth's heartbeat wakes us.

The Oppression Tables: Genesis

      Black
is not the desired color
of women

      Black
is too loud it needs a touch
of something to mute her
boisterous nature

      Black
is not the desired color
for women

bible is black bible is not
monogamous

but bible wants her to love
him only & bible will only
promise love at gunpoint

greyhound bus station 1950

Bea
the gift shop's salesclerk
wore the scent of virginia
on her feet
she walked hard

like farmhands do but she
was beginning to understand
northern habituals

going to beauty shops
buying greens at food barn
dropping her ah rahs

but jim crow wouldn't leave her alone
he kept showing up when she
tried on sassy chartreuse hats
with 9 inch feathers bowed around
the brim (for wednesday 5 o'clock service
at enon baptist)

lucky brown cosmetics
reddish savoy pumps at florine's
the may company's policy did not allow
grease stains on the merchandise
so she stepped over to sapphire's brims
we crown colored heads

at the station she left the change for white
customers on the counter black skin leaches
yet her pride was in the display:
travels with white aunts
see new york city on a dollar a day

but she knew her station
arrived here at 19 to attend a colored
school for colored women

the stationmaster felt a colored salesclerk
would better serve their customers as
a domestic in the back like her ride
up south

In Virginia

In Virginia's room
Her own
Peruvian lilies light her desk
With carefully placed pens
Bought with her own words
The groovings in the desk waxed by
Pearline who at noon serves Earl Grey
In a pink apron carrying pink teacups
Laced with lemon on its pungent lip
Delicate woman-sized treats for swooning
Pearline moves to the door to bring in the Silk Road porcelain tub
Camphor, salts, and tints-of-violet to balm Virginia's tuckered feet
Unbend the curvature of Virginia's back the enamored covetous prose
In Virginia's own
Pearlie she calls *bring my notebooks and more tea*
Pearline walks hard into the kitchen to draw the fires prepare domesticity
For the writer who needs a room of her own to subordinate her muse
Her maid who labors for Miss Virginia's ownness, her roominess
Virginia says the room frees her from the tyranny of man
Her men, planters and industrialists
Pearline is asked to stay late to prepare refreshments for her writer friends

To collect their wet coats and dry them by the hearth

And pleasantly waitress their personalities

Pearline agreeable prepares the table embosses it with fairies

and musing mermaids tapered flickering

Nights when Pearline walks to her bus stop fresh from clanking silver goblets of drink

She has never tasted goes to the butcher for the leftover shanks of meat closest to

The guts of its porcine body for her own family's stewed victuals

At home she draws the fire for her children's nightly bath

Washes clothes for school on the morrow, braids their hair

After all and sundry has been cared for she walks to the pallet she shares

And thinks of Virginia's ownness the ownness that she

Pearline keeps pristine from the tyranny of mistress Virginia's men

Drylongso

she seen't mz cinda selfpossessing
blackening windows at sittin' up she
li/ke/ded sapphire wimmins
sassing dem duppies

she burned her crown of thorns sent
for from jesus's estate &
laid it at mz mary magdalene's fi/nal/ity
without the holy ghost she ain't no sisyphus

back in the day she & her grrrls dey broke jesus
out of dat cleft he be washing her feet e/tern/ity

the kelley women: a story of africans and romas

my mother was afraid of romas
whenever she encountered the parlors
with the tinted signs tarots read here or
a pink neon handprint etched with blue lettering
proclaiming madam z cures afflictions and
removes jumbies from any dwelling
she'd remind me of her rearing up
in kilmarnock and the *gypsies* as she puts it
would camp out on their land with tents
boiling cauldrons rickety trucks carrying
loads of roma-essence they preferred to camp out
back along the flower fairies and tree lilies
mz cinda had instilled fear what kind of white
folks camp on a colored person's land by this
time the kelley men had long left no traces of
manhood or folk men about the place my mother and
her mother mae would peep about the encampment
when the romas went to town to sell fortunes
the fortune-tellers were a threat to those who believed in jesus and hoodoo
they feared their spells may have more strength than the
african obeah but the dark hair and the dark white skin my mother
said could be a sign of colored influence mz cinda reckoned
these spell makers may be weaker because of this miscegenated power but they
beared watching
my mother bea mae's daughter found a strange colored doll
which they attempted to give in friendship but history taught
her *different* no they *beared* watching from the house up by the road
just in case

and we'll understand it better bye and bye

*

mz cinda's slipper room
affixed along a tripod of
plants that "grow up with no
masters" halts
desert affinities
blooms willow womanness

*

mz cinda custodian of mountain water slips of pods,
tree products from virginia's guitar hills prizes buffalo
clover and latticed rootings a skein of peruvian fairies
and tulip pinks sprawl yon and gilt the overlays of vine
and verbena

*

mae lays mz cinda's braids to fan across the small of her
working back   twists an orange coil at the tips dried from
peeled oranges it scents the darkened room she smells the
seeds that sowed them

*

and directs mae to add chandeliers of bloodgrass elijah's wife comes
by to bring patterned shells for mz cinda to paint by the numbers
elijah's wife an apostle like the santero women of her clan removes from her sack
a burnished oil to unrankle the skin about mz cinda's eyes

*

mz cinda whistles as she moors her feet deeper into the clay floor whistles
deeper as her song meanders about
her jesus in the sweet bye and bye

Black and Blue

today I am 54
in a smallish room
that has a used bed
a featherless down comforter circa 1954

my swelling feet are propped
against a tasseled pillow that says
God bless our home

there is an old box that
plays Autumn in New York
and I pour another nip

later I may look for an all-night cafeteria
with an all you can eat buffet
I have long since given up on one-plate specials
I eat alone for the pleasure and
the pain
it is now night fall
and the voice pitches the same
blue note
as it was then in 1942

colored and colorated
I reach over
pull the chain on the light
and pray that if I wake that
I am not lonesome
tonight

The Disowning.

When my mother left

you narrowed.

There was that nasty business of my eviction

from your hallowed home.

The spleen you used to brand me the convenient

forgettery of my deliverance from your witch camps

its filigree of insignificance my rusted birth thickened by

the gin of being, "pain covered with skin."

porch stories

the plum yews
catch the lights of the lean-to
its tintinnabulation of phallic branches
like a skipping 45 record
as my grandmother pounds coarsened cornmeal
tends to her pot of mustards and dandelions
her camphorated feet in my grandfather's brown slippers
the thwack thwack on the cement floor
the spasms of roiling water ready for mint tea and biscuits
jars of blackberry preserves and bluefish from last night
she scrapes butter from the dish onto my plate
and i lick the creamy sweet
swirl my tongue around the circumference
of my mouth   i swoon
it's like juju beans and popcorn from her bag at the show
the yews hush and
i go out to the porch
to look at the sheen of buttercups under my chin
i place my hand over the water jar
to watch the marquee of lightning bugs
decorated with bishop's lace and blush

my grandparents once bought me a bow and arrow

for my birthday and i run and squawk chasing the flamboyant

rooster peacocking in the yard his crown like petals

today is my grandmother's day off

from jefferson's carpet factory

on seaman's road

in arkadelphia

the banner of fiberglass   burned into her hands

the burrs in her stoop

the scabrous lungs

the din of unplumbed air

the inked bone

at 8.10 an hour for a living wage

colored hats

a type of mirror discriminates   behind absence stumbles a power   conflicts jerk black room before spoiled milk   black room conforms   toes the line next to the owed truth how does the black room perceive an item   why can't   black room shove the living mercury   black rooms without closures   listen moral   a dogma sickens underneath black room cues outside its box   barrels a tunnel   a policeman explodes   the heart smells through any bay   burnt air guides a groan   how does black room pale with the poetic sunrise   black room revolts against the eagle

segregated blood

we women sit
in bald yards
among the ozone dried
laundry
plaiting brittle
hair red and patchy
at the side door
yardbirds peck perversely
at shimmers
from the back
of someone's throat
we no longer read the water
its brutish blue is hemlock
the nigrescence
of the mississippi
is sullen and lowdown
from our quarters
the day smells of
cinnamon and corn cakes
mixed with the whiffing hack
of car batteries
on balustrades
of tract homes
we pick at the scorched
cayenne and tubers
slap at the muddy slaughter
of buttercups and bean fields
miss(is) the old settler's
beastly whiteness on black

the lengua of cotton and auctions
compelling baths cannot repair
the industrial birth
yoked in idiotic trees
fluorescent
unbranched
the shackled earth faints
fears the vanished view
the dying bell is prepared
we women look for poultices
to catch babies from
cloven wombs from
infected nights
in tupelo's
culm and crop
in the looking
we discover
the absence of
blood

negroesbuyahouse

the collective whisper began on april 2, 1965 in the 1400 east independence avenue on the truck a family of four transporting housewares various & sundry negrobilia along with heavy chintz furniture with knotted plastic coverings the collective neighbors catty-corner to shaded windows elongated green telephone cords on rotary phones signaling to their neighbors that what they had overheard at the local woolworth's was indeed true each neighbor waited with the newest of negro detectors these negroes had mobbed into montgomery heights like swarms of roaches roaches bred 2,000 at a time in secret colonies one neighbor even swore that she saw the heads of the polk family over on america crossroads in the eddy of a fiery cauldron for sale signs flapped furiously atop newly dug sod by noon a transformation had occurred the family toting britannica encyclopedias a red and white mica kitchen set & 1959 blue chevy was officially a ghetto

little negro lyes
for Akilah Oliver

eye

lye

when i lift

      porcelana

to bland

         my senses

scrubbing veiled

    new grow skin.

        i am

madgehestic's daughter

      within my

      dome

      things

          fall

        apart i'd

(re)imagining hattie

i imagine god to be hattie mcdaniel in she floral apron
mistaking me scarlet and hot combing my roots

i tries to tell she i'm colored me but she keeps banjoing dixie

i imagine mammy frying hotwater cornbread, hamhocked dandelion greens
swilling cool mint juleps seized from dem done gone with dey wind

tenderizing braids what needs its kitchen greezed, parting waves & oiling ash

i imagine hattie mcdaniel spreading she thighs to honeysuckle all she chirrens
waiting for dat blackened hebben we got when dey jesus was exiled to u rope.

this here aint a allen ginsberg poem!

for the bondswomen at the corner of 138TH and willis ave who begin each day with lord
please don't let me haveta who raise 9 kids and 4 grands without leave who prone beg
prison guards to release her sanitary pads who as mule of the world make a drop to cop
who make change at any laundromat & any cafeteria who leave the lite on & hopes her
sons will not be stopped by 5-o who quote malcolm in howard beach who remind me
where i came from & why i will return whose lyricism is memoried in muh dear's back
who read by remembering the shapes who write by tracing them who make biscuits
with lard & buttermilk who swell from diabetic sores who on sundays wears a peacock
feather in her crown who are blinded by ms justice flinging her headlong through steel
scales leaving tattoos of the TRIANGULAR TRADE who collect bottles of love & acid & sell
them side by side whose still van der zee is hottentot & maisha around the way whose
gaze leave that well of loneliness who be badu but cries like nina who wake up on the 9th
month of mother's day & burns his shit whose beloved mama is etched in stone who bleed
without cycle & drinks straight no chaser when she conjure bessie & get brittney whose
genesis is her exodus who bind meatloaf with utz potato chips who buy pickled pigs' feet
pickled eggs & lil' debbies @ the bodega for a dollar who at jesus will save you church of
god in christ pledge her allegiance to the holy ghost whose power is living in spite of who
go where everyone is her friend but no one is my poem bes a bluespoem for the sistahs at
the corner of ahunnard and thirtyeighth and will/is

Forgotten Negroes: Hospital for the Negro Insane

he was not a universal man
he was a negro man
a negro chauffeur

in Crownsville
in the stubborn light
itinerant negro boxer

he appeared white
until he opened his negro suit/case
and unpacked the negrobilia

articles of negro insanity:
an Ethiop arcade photo
negro photos of freedom
a hard pressed military uniform
with negro insignias
negro baby shoes
a negro starter gun
2 negro letters to kin in
West Virginia

1946: they took him
because his negro meal
was served on a broken plate
his negro anger had a negro male
diagnosis
paranoid schizophrenic: negro man
                                        with a cause
recollections: Mr Frank (last name lost in scuffle)
            negro job as boy or case #3997 on his negro cross in 1984
resisted

roun' kilmarnock way

and tha kelley wimmins bake
dey corn cakes serve may wine on
low country
for kilmarnock sistren

mz cinda lost location roun' she
eyes inquires bout a baldhead
when suckin she teef gal where
mae mz cinda's daughter
shushes

mz cinda she on de poach
mz cinda she not be silenced

confounded she *ah rah* where she baldhead mz cinda be laughin ah reckon

she no hear

de screen in me window

Persistence of Memory

lucinda, the grrrl before a mirror
behind a low narrow basin
leans into the watery reflection
and observes the buckles of
scar tissue shaped like petals of blood
there's a photo of her on the table
standing alongside her kindred
amid a menagerie of winecups
she looks sideways at her grandbaby
in lace, her husband clematis
slightly turned with a black spade
as mae her oldest looks straight ahead
with her chin on lucinda's shoulder
her hand cupping the baby's frame
unfinished revolutions lie fallow
under a canopy of cypress trees
heels crush skulls bloodfruit imprints
the landscape dna leaches into birchbark
flesh peels back and white hot ash falls away
marrow pools its roots
your tongue repeats hymns
summons phantom slave souls razored into their collective memory
the autumn in kilmarnock persists induces blue apple leaves
the dandy of roasted potatoes and corn
you store sleeves of perch and porgies
line kasai velvet in hat boxes in concert with knitted furies of weather and wane
the swell of cimarron horses load and lop in fields
abreast the heft and hate of their masters the wind circles back
retraces and blows past your images on that crystalline table
but the photo conceals the others waiting in groves
facing your land and your cocked pistol   deep

act so there is no use in a centre.

words like negroes
must be in season
not too dark

kin to a white cousin
like monet's water lilies

black is politic
it casts too many shadows
trying to be adjacent to the sun

black words
like a black dog
may foam or fang
or
! penetrate
cut their straps
from boots
and strangle the language

Black Persists

Black steams the current cosmology without a biblical machine /a paradox spasm / politics within a banjo binds the dishonest imperative /the ground treks beneath the seabell /the ancient symmetry /a spur persists against its opposite /tongues scandalize the union /speaks the theater of colored ways /interprets the lisps of the sorry demise /water fountains disordered colored /how will the river tame slaves /slaves buried underneath the constitution /the past flowers into fire /a lie overwhelms a correct inheritance /boats imprison Black within the hired angle /the century betrays colored /allocates a rabid crowd inside a persistent settled memory /the truth belongs to persistence before persistence changes memory /every skin illustrates memory /the retired rage reposes against the hardy slue /trees pulse in the rose rain /can this illegal contract purchase trees /hanging holds trees /trees collapse beneath the terrible orbit /bone disturbs light a gloaming in the assaulted geography /why won't hate smell his warped horror /tongues misinterpret a seen monopoly /night deletes /night corrects shade/night teaches shade after the immense dawn /forced beds clang under the sick age /sun changes the unwise crop /memory tools the oar

Florence.

Florence.
Collects other charred lives,
their jilted tatters with coffee stains,
held inside a closed purse with a large safety
pin. Stashed replicas of nondescript,
imaginaries on cardboard canvasses.

Her cast of selves is parenthetical, vexing audiences who cannot look away. She favors
GPC cigarettes. Smoky coils cluster her brown-shining fingernails with fleshy residue,
which she monotonously plucked out of her face.

Florence (Lee) once said she birthed herself
inthatdumpsteronmainstreetinwestminster &
only she could undo it.

Negro-related Conditions

1.
in my parents' country at 5 a.m.
my father swings his legs over
the bed planks
clasps the fissures in his turgid knuckles
for 22,580 days through each abusive season
he thinks it is the american dream
spored nigrescent lips
canaries at his feet

2.
my mother rises too
at 5 a.m.
to cook his grits
pack a cold sandwich
a small apple for sweet
it is almost time for her bath
she's the cafeteria lady at my school

3.
last night in my parents' country
there were no darling dears
quiet talks about the children
no locked embraces or patted behinds
only creaking steps the snuffing of fires
an occasional proximity of

south

trains patent satchels
regret digs
a century demands the imbalance   the inflamed geography
a worrying sector crows jim
jim crow blacks behave inside a skull
should god rail opposite the inflexible kind
a consent buses a turnaround
painted bigotry proceeds across the conditioned ground
bible experiments with Africa
Africa opens bible
Africa waits for the wealth opposite the bible
the bible washes Africa before the atomic skin
under bible burns the aligning tribes
Africa gasps

The Hunger Season

pecked into
the shape of lips
the white resin of
starvation
our daily bread

licks the maple of fibrous sod
chews the meat of skeleton
wings and carcasses

our tongues hold in its
faucets
elusive water
the nativity of bread and wine
the vague flowering of grain
in the false light
its trace and aura
in the head of my head
is the secret architecture
of rice and bread
the flutter tonguing
from lack
the dry folds of undersides

the last sweet remembrance
of dates and cassava
in Ouagadougou and Tupelo
the ligatures of hunger are
white as the asp in faun
500 years
the intended genocide
upon her furled petals of humanity

all the bushmen's horses

i am too busy looking for food to think about peace my gun
is how i support my family i watch my neighbors turn to ash
as janjaweed on camels kill our teachers

my children black at a school   days
after arab teachers left before the carnage

too many horsemen murahaleen at the nuba mountains
south is black and slave and infidel darfur cattlekeepers,
farmworkers, domestics
women and children pledged as gifts to berbers baggaras

in our sudan land of the blacks people shout
for rain to stop the
burn of skin against skin
i did not like protesting   or
the crouching anger it is not a recent
thing
all the bushmen's horses
it is personal
they force us to have sex with our fathers   the plot
where my mother lives burned yesterday
gunshots and ululations

                    the road out
leaves behind fallen home fronts errant livestock
old men with carts pushing makeshift chifforobes
charred tires and trash a wooden chair a doorknob a grrrl's
plastic belt a child's cheaply colored pillow a shirt turned
brown from too much blood and shit a watery shaped
imprint of a shadow spreads the stubbled upholstery of
clothes

i carry my mother's soiled body we leave
without our voices
we only have stones

they have all the power
no one ever listens to
us . . .

6 million cremated   silence burns fur
4 more years they shout across the atlantic

The Color of Remembrance

her mind holds a seashell, its drone of
passage, whir, whispers the incessant rolling
in and out of disturbed wavelets, the speed
of sound the clanking bows and lurching
peace

the crowds of shackled hosts at the edges of
battened sails the lean-to freedom, to the
passion of shark's teeth, the ecstasy of water
the eternal sleep of Africa

the sound and fury of a mind trapped in
the dysmembered tribes someone must be
the host for the Africans who walked on
water

A Day of Grace

On the morning of Grace's death
I saw her at the community latrine
showering her baby grrrls.

At Makola Market #2 buying
coal and a miniature packet of rice beneath
the burning war clouds like red lanterns on a promenade.

They were looking for water among
the vernal pyre of rot, the roux of human salt.
In the ambivalent allness of war and freedom

Grace once told me that there was no photograph or
memory of her in a camera with the Eye of Ra shining
on the pluck of a small African grrrl in the moorlands,
a grace of a grrrl.

Later, I heard from my neighbor, Aleke, that Grace had been disposed of
in the knotty fields where she searched for burnt water,
identified by the stains on her skirt
when her children went to the fields to collect her.

The government told them, "Sorry."
"It was the word *sorry* you used when you have burned a pot."

Give me your bloodied pudenda, your *Amistad*

Your guns yearning to blast freedom

As it removes the wretched bigly labor from our alt-shores

Send these, your covfefe to my Russian man

I lift America great, as jim crows, her golden door

To *the People of Iraq: What You Can Expect from America in* 2007

what we seeing is
the streets, the cops, the system, the harassment,
the options, get shot, go to jail, or getcha ass kicked
DMX

dear fatima:

keisha here   grrrl you don't know me but i felt i should write & drop some science your
way about what you can expect now that you have become a people in captivity   they will
remove the burqa & put a noose around your neck as the rockets red glare   god fearing
people will ask their god to enslave yours for 500 years & brand you inferior shiftless and a
lazy picaninny you will have the distinction of being the "sand n*****s" of kingdom come

the military is there to make sure you have no health care food housing you know the
survivals & all that shit people of the world should have except the designated negroes
prepare to hear your child cry from hunger & ignorance   you will be denied substantial
portions of bread rice and water but you will have a heavy diet of bullets & democratic
poverty even the oil that belongs to you is a lie   you will be told you stole the oil from
america   you are a people without a country without a language without a culture without
a country   iraqi money will go from saddam to sadubya   the constitution   your
constitution will be rewritten by dubya said document will declare that you are 60% human

if you're not used to voting well america won't disappoint the shack & shackles are
your mainstay but gnash no matter how useless   forget mike be like harriet & build an

underground railroad, read nat turner's insurrection 101 he may help you on nights like these

stay steady like malcolm   i know yall got your peoples & all but i just wanted to speak about how we got ovah   there was this here sister sister anna julia cooper who said when & where i enter the whole race enters with me   i have to sleep by these words nightly or i would . . .

well im sure this letter is being read by the govvamint so ive got to watch my back there are folks who have been incarcerated for decades for speaking too loudly ive gotta coupla kids i gotta feed but i will hip you another time   remember, no matter how many times daily you make salat   allah won't be living there anymore

the hierarchy of humanity

we rotate
luminous on the muddy
rubes bright beside the
dreamscape a free so
violet against the intended
fog i am sensuous before
the auction while the
crowd watched on jubilee
we are humming against
this land the birth is hard
all arid within the skin of
restraints i violate and
redden the hierarchy of
humanity

And It Is the Presence

in our ancient familiar
of dunes and sea
foregrounding
the sparest of fainted auras
the breasts of ships mired in sin
the seduction of human scurf into hazes of
living waters
totems of everyday molderings under
native grasses wild sour oranges mariposas
ponderosa pines and duckweed
and yawp of faunal settlements in flames
the planed-away shapes of eights and limbs
dragged dry as cotton on our backs in the ball of cloven suns
the physiognomy of bondage
daring the bartered peace
of meager gods

A Social Worker in Black

Two boys in the back seat sucking on hard candy shifting and rolling, eye signals. Mom,
next to me complaining about the ninth move to yet

another institution for the permanently poor. As stones swirl, gravel catches, the
blowing trash hits the windshield, we realize with jerking

heads that this be it. Later, I went to check on them and the boys were sleeping on the
plastic mats alongside walls that said,

This place is a hellhole, yo mama, and fuck you, Keisha.
As I adjusted to the dimness I knew mama was gone

I checked the facility, the cold, even tree caves.
She was gone and gone.

The next morning as I fed the boys, I wondered what to do.
The boys did not ask of her nor were they particularly different.

I paced all day. I had never called child protective services.
I have always found a way to get around such nasty matters, like

abandonment. Child protective services arrived at 6 p.m. in a light blue sedan with dark
seats. Some sort of bland seal on its side. City of New York. I had been holding the boys
for the past 24 hours, they were my flesh now.

I approached the workers and said I would look after them until their mother returned.
Perhaps she had been hurt or lost her way.

She didn't know the area. The workers looked past me to the boys. One of them went to their room to place their survivals in a large dark green trash bag. You know, the kind with the steel handles.

I held them and I told the 7-year-old that he must stay with his 3-year-old brother. Go to school and never split up. Stay together, I said, Stay together. I held them by the shoulders, and I whispered, STAY TOGETHER.

And keep my number in your pants pocket. As they sat in the back seat never talking, never signaling, only looking at the headrests on the front seat, I motioned to the 7-year-old to roll down the window. Hold Jahi's hand, Malik.

I step forward as they pull off. I see that Malik puts his hand in Jahi's, eyes straight ahead.

we are children they gave us out like chickens
destroyed our vision burnt 'til nothing was there set
upon by those who killed our parents made us sleep
with them before they died tethered to our blood and
piss splattered vestures my voice knuckled in my
clotted tongue and pieces spill atop rock hewn by
skull i rub where i can't see each brown tinged
peeling of skin like stripped bark
i ask them to "beat the slavery right out of me"
it is the same
war and peace
killing small children made it a smaller sin.

Africans unearthed beneath wall street

base of the belly's tethered voices
lunge at the spearing of huddled graves

rice husks cover concentric plats
of fermented burial grounds quickly left behind

after pearl harvest the night before emancipation Africa cleaves
bonded wall street   below

trading platforms spur the opening clang
9 a.m. reminders of acquisition   human lading in any century

new york life ensures bess, negress, deeded to mistress
sa-rah for her natural life and 500 for unnatural

loss of wages: cleft limbs at birth, escape, purposeful poisoning,
and reading

here below the towers, baldwin's epitaph
"the fire next time."

at the five-mile house
roasted meats and johnnie walker black served by gap-
toothed maids to the neighborhood elite big willie and
nem spin joshua redman some new kind of flavva it
ain't no juke but it be real close and the only hip is in
the bop
still five on the black hand side

The Taxidermy of Grrrl Black

Sometimes in the sea's haze I can make out his silhouette. He wears a dark jacket and jeans, hair cut short to the scalp. I try to imagine his eyes but only the corneas appear. I close in. It is then he erases the space between us. He captures me I am stuck. Stuck in the spaces he has drawn me into. I am frozen. An elusive mist, nothingness in the power he blunts over my marked body. I cannot see him. He can see me, the physicality of me. He empties me and I feel as though I have slumped forward onto his hisness. I don't know what he is made of. I just feel frozen. I won't flee. Sometimes flight is not an option. Just the wind of being restrained in captivity. He uses his voice. He uses his voice to weaponize and it works. I retreat. I am frozen. When I appear to thaw even slightly, sweat thru the ice, he uses his voice. But I didn't move fast enough, wasn't sufficiently fearful and he showed it. He said he didn't want to, but I didn't do what he told me to do. I said no, I would never. But I think that I said it to myself. My voice sank, sank into the bodice of me. My lips are frozen so I am not speaking to him. I am only speaking to the shell I have carved myself into. I have hardened so he cannot penetrate my exterior. I don't know how to protect me from what he has promised. He has weaponized the moment. He has shown it to me. It is arched and has notches and a machined touch the way he cocks it. I figure out how to breathe without him hearing me. I cannot see him. I cannot let him see me see him. I turn my head to the side of me. I invisible. I invisible myself. I contort into smallness. I am not small, yet I can shapeshift. Weapons always mirror the hand it magnifies and all that is left is that which is meant to murder to maim to make you suicide the person you used to be.

Comes the Colored Hour

I do not have any more candles
It has now been detected   Blood is a
soothsayer I do not believe in
predispositions   Especially in the color
Black

I won't caress it   Cannot turn my back on
it either   It rearranges itself

Will hit you over the head & you
fall to a leaning
Its origin: a jane crow hue

Revelation: I have always been here
Maybe it is me
But it has been known to hide with its

curled teeth and waifish gills
I do not trust you
I will rely on my insides

I am afraid of that arc of Nothingness I cannot relive
that lived life
The hallowed chambers will be Home

Home is an impenetrable kiln or a guitar-shaped container
I do not want to be contained
There has always been some law
Some someone who has hemmed me within this thread
No edges to jump from just the aught of   I will be
forgotten except maybe fleetingly

They have gotten over my leave-taking   No matter what
they say it is by force
They will say that I have lived a long lush life

I will now be attached to platitudes perhaps a song
It will be said that blue is my favorite color oxtails my go-to
That I prefer the fragrances of sweet peas butter beans the sachets of

lavender roses   A eulogy in a few words or less will do an accounting I have
never caressed so many (dead) flowers   Hymns play on autopilot on an organ a
creepy dirge of love

It is dirt or pyre
And then folks will throw the last wildflower on where they think I may be
Turn and go back to the salt of their lives   Banal thoughts on what to serve
for dinner & the clothes at the
Laundromat since you are wearing your last clean pair of drawers.

let them be named

a pitcher fallen across a clothed table partially hides a series
of stained notes composed with a hurried pen the bearer
writes of secret passions amongst interleavings she smears
a serum of directions where to find the disfigurement left
under a palette of nettings and oddments its face is partially
covered by the afterbirth the umbilicus is astride a body
now an encasement of tissue and membrane elijah's wife the
bearer is muted by the imperfection she discarded among
the ruins inside her name her authentic clan of women

Her Marked Black Body

the macabre moon
once lunged at me
it hisses red
hangs voyeuristically
wants me to stand in its balkanized light

such a pyretic massacre
will keep her paralyzed yonder
Black combs and a vexed vulva
clotted in grimy knurls for the
perilous public

i figured it out
the amber has been interfered with
no one will be coming
she will dissolve in rodent grasses she is not
missing

she is dead yet there is a handsome trail of Black
crumbs glued in bloodied quicksand it is a lunar
uprising unbound by the neighborhood's

sinister grama the moon antiquates time it is
elusive such light won't guard you so stand your
ground

Belly of
      the Black moon
            shapes the ninth muse

Acknowledgments

I wish to thank the editors of the following publications:

Black Warrior Review: "The History of Gynecology" and "Then I Will Speak on the Ashes"; *Bellevue Literary Review*: "Her Marked Black Body" and "The Taxidermy of Grrrl Black"; *Kweli*: "My Mother the Lunch Lady"; *Black Nature: Four Centuries of African American Nature Poetry*: "potters' field"; *Nocturnes 3: (re)view of the literary arts*: "Erasures of History," "weather report," and "Drylongso"; *Tuesday; An Art Project*: "Forgotten Negroes: Hospital for the Negro Insane"; *Yellow Medicine Review*: "porch stories," "segregated blood," and "act so there is no use in a centre"; *The Ringing Ear: Black Poets Lean South*: "the kelley women: a story of africans and romas"; *Mythium Literary Journal*: "Daughters of Harriet"; *Dudley Review*: "Negro-related conditions"; *Crab Orchard Review*: "Prevalence of Ritual"; *The Black Arts Quarterly: Stanford University*: "black persists," "[forced beds . . .]," and "[at the five mile house . . .]"; *x magazine* (flipped eye publishing): "this here ain't a allen ginsberg poem" and "all the bushmen's horses"

A fervent thank you to my editor Stephanie G'Schwind, who has made this process seamless and supported my views and imperfections. She provided a safe vessel to a wayfaring woman. I owe a tremendous debt to Brenda Hillman, my mentor and friend, who has read and provided the lantern I needed through several iterations of my work with grace and love as a much-needed lifeline. Brenda has been in my life through some of the most difficult and joyous periods and has always remained the same wondrous person. And to Rai Ahmed-Green for her hours of work on my manuscript. I wish to thank Crystal Simone Smith, publisher of Backbone Press for publishing my chapbook, *Drapetomania,* and Camille Dungy, who has supported my work and opened a possibility to an eventuality. Many thanks to Megan Lear, to whom I am indebted for designing such a wondrous cover, and to copyeditor C. E. Janecek, typesetter Patrick Carey, and proofreader Sara Hughes for tending to the care of my words. Thank you to Tara Betts, Kiki Petrosino, Tongo Eisen-Martin, Crystal Wilkinson, Chet'la Sebree, CM Burroughs, Lauren K. Alleyne, Taylor Johnson, and Brandee Younger, who all lifted me up and read my work without hesitation. I am thankful for the advice and warmth from Patricia Smith, who also made a way for me at Vermont College of Fine Arts. Thank you to Rickey Laurentiis for inspiring "The History of Gynecology." I would like to posthumously thank Jan Doane of Saint Mary's College for her ways of seeing me. Thanks also to Jessica Hagedorn, who does not know that many years ago she ignited the spark that started me on this voyage after she confronted me at a workshop in East Harlem. I would like to recognize Honorée Fanonne Jeffers, who graciously offered to help me obtain a residency and followed my work. I owe a debt of gratitude to Meta DuEwa Jones, who encouraged me to pursue an MFA and supported me during the application process. My thanks to Dominic Ripoli, who guided me during this process. I am grateful to Hanmin and Jennifer Liu of Wildflowers of San Francisco, the San Francisco Foundation/Nomadic Press for visibility, and the Nomadic Press Poetry Prize and the judges Tongo Eisen-Martin, Devorah Major, and Kim Shuck, Poets Laureate of San Francisco. To Edna DeCoursey Johnson and Ruth Saulesbury, who really saw me and nurtured the awkward grrrlBlack whose joy was in lifting the pen to tell stories about Black Lives. I cannot forget Amiri Baraka, who gave me encouragement and a blanket during our workshop and became known to this day as the Baraka blanket, a metaphor for protection when writing as an outrider. I would like to acknowledge the Hurston-Wright Foundation, my first writers conference, where I discovered that being a Blackwomanwriter is woven into my identity. I cannot forget my ancestors who perished in the Middle Passage and endured the brutality as enslaved people, so that I could become an amanuensis through which they could testify. An enduring and spiritual thank you to Harriet Tubman and Ida B. Wells, who are the goalposts for Black women's lives matter. This book is especially dedicated to my mother, Dorothy Beatrice Parker (Kelley), who is responsible for the making of this book, for my lifetime love of the written word, and who never for a moment imagined me to be anything other than worthy; my father, Franklin Roosevelt Parker; my grandmother Mary Curry Kelley; sista Diane Newsome; and my great-grandmother Lucinda Curry, whose stories about the Kelley women were braided into my existence and recounted by my mother throughout my life and are the basis for this book. And finally, to my daughter, Briana, who is the meaning of life. Also, to my grandson, Bear, whose Black boy joy and brilliance is as bright as his beauty.

This book is set in Sabon
by The Center for Literary Publishing
at Colorado State University.

Copyediting by C. E. Janecek.
Proofreading by Sara Hughes.
Book design and typesetting by Patrick Carey.
Cover design by Megan Lear.
Printing by Bookmobile.